Meaningful MATH

Creating an Environment with Math-Rich Experiences

Written by Jeri A. Carroll

Illustrated by Janet Armbrust

Teaching & Learning Company

1204 Buchanan St., P.O. Box 10
Carthage, IL 62321-0010

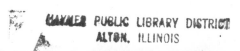

This book belongs to

_____

Cover photo by Images and More Photography

Copyright © 1999, Teaching & Learning Company

ISBN No. 1-57310-191-5

Printing No. 987654321

Teaching & Learning Company
1204 Buchanan St., P.O. Box 10
Carthage, IL 62321-0010

Table of Contents

Dear Teacher or Parent,

Why is it so important to provide meaningful math experiences for young children, in classrooms and at home? What can young children learn about math anyway? Will they be doing addition and subtraction worksheets in preschool and kindergarten? First and second grade? Does *developmentally appropriate practice* mean to put away the math experiences until children are ready? No, actually it means to provide meaningful math experiences for children of any age or stage, wherever those experiences can be meaningful. The National Council of Teachers of Mathematics (NCTM) believes that early childhood math programs for young children 3-8 should be developmentally appropriate.

NCTM's position is that math instruction for young children should incorporate active and interactive learning experiences, recognizing that young children's understandings develop as they "explore, investigate and discuss mathematical concepts." The classroom environment should provide for the study of mathematics in an on-going fashion with those concepts "integrated with other subject areas, making use of natural connections whenever they occur." It is up to the teachers to provide experiences where children can "repeatedly experience through concrete, visual, verbal and pictorial formats" the mathematical concepts they are ready for. What better way than to provide a math-rich environment, an environment where children learn through observation, exploration, verbalization and hands-on experiences. A combination of playful experiences and meaningful math instruction provides the best possible influence on children's mathematical development. That's why a book about creating a meaningful math environment for the early childhood classroom.

Sincerely,

Jeri

Jeri A. Carroll

Turn your room into an alive learning environment and make math meaningful! It's easy to start simply by decorating the walls, bulletin boards, shelves and tabletops with colorful numbers and shapes as you teach beginning skills in counting, measuring, telling time, money and writing numbers.

Make children aware when you use math meaningfully. Let the children watch as you tally the number of lunches; compute book club orders; count money for a class trip; and check the time for your weekly visit to the library, art room or music teacher. As your students see you use math in a meaningful manner, they too will attempt similar activities.

This book provides a variety of ideas, techniques and strategies to use to encourage young children to learn about math. It contains several sections with checklists, activities and reproducibles that will help make your students inquisitive, creative and competent.

Materials

Add meaningful math materials to existing centers whenever possible. Even at a reading center, you can use math by posting the date a book is due back at the library. Mark the date on a class calendar and refer to the calendar daily.

Numbers, Number Words and Sets

Have several sets of large, easy-to-read, colorful numbers, number words and counting charts that all children can see from different parts of the room.

Exploring Math Concepts

Capture appropriate learning moments when children can explore numbers. Note the time rain starts and stops and figure out how long it rained; count the number of umbrellas in the room on a rainy day; bring attention to the use of numbers when you read aloud. Count the number of windows on the school bus, have children notice the license numbers on their parents' cars and count how many cars are in the school parking lot. The motivating possibilities are all around.

ABOUT THIS BOOK

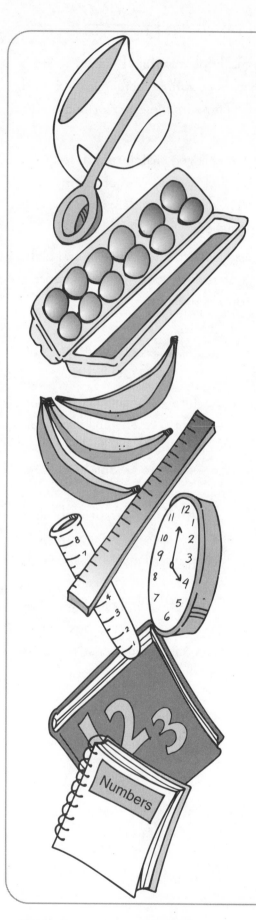

Numbers for Units

Add math activities to your class units. Children love classroom cooking and it provides perfect opportunities for measuring.

Making Math Books

Make your own number, shape, time, measurement and money books.

Ads and Catalogs

Provide materials and supplies so children can make their own ads and catalogs.

What Comes in 1s, 2s and 3s?

Look for things that come in pairs, sixes and dozens. How many eggs come in a carton? How many sticks of butter come in a package? Are there always the same number of bananas in a bunch?

Clip-and-Copy Measures and Activities

Use the clip-and-copy measures to provide children realistic representations of measuring tools. Make charts and activity cards for students using these reproducibles.

Math Portfolios

Save activities, pictures, photographs, etc., to put in children's portfolios to document math activities.

Books, Books, Books

Become familiar with new books for young children about numbers and number concepts. It's a perfect way for children to learn reading and math at the same time!

Environmental Materials
Recognizing and Reading Numbers

It's easy to make math come alive when you use a variety of learning tools to teach new skills. Look over the following lists and check off those materials you already have in your classroom. Next, check with your school math center and your district science center to see what is available on a borrowing basis. Finally, make a list of those materials not available and make plans to purchase or order them.

Recognizing and Reading Numbers

- [ ] pocket chart and number cards
- [ ] plastic number tiles
- [ ] number concentration cards
- [ ] overhead number boards
- [ ] magnetic numbers
- [ ] individual number lines
- [ ] number/set cards
- [ ] overhead number tiles
- [ ] number boards
- [ ] magnetic board
- [ ] class number line

Environmental Materials
Number Writing

Provide plenty of materials so children can write numbers in meaningful ways. If they aren't yet writing, make sure there are stamps and sticker numbers.

Check your room for these. If you don't have them, place a requisition next year.

Number Writing

- ☐ ink pads
- ☐ chalkboards
- ☐ number cards
- ☐ pencils and pens
- ☐ markers
- ☐ paper
- ☐ number stamps

- ☐ chalk
- ☐ number word cards
- ☐ crayons
- ☐ adding machine tape
- ☐ scratch pads
- ☐ sticky notes

Environmental Materials
Learning to Count and Compute

When children begin to add, it won't be in their heads. It will be with meaningful materials. Make sure that you have plenty of things to count. Remember, it is a lot more interesting to count pennies than beads.

Check your room for these. If you don't have them, place a requisition next year.

Learning to Count and Compute

- ☐ dominoes
- ☐ counter tubs and bowls
- ☐ calculators
- ☐ inchworms
- ☐ buttons
- ☐ beads
- ☐ teddy bear counters
- ☐ dice
- ☐ bingo
- ☐ spinners
- ☐ tongue depressors
- ☐ cubes
- ☐ overhead inchworms
- ☐ soft plastic counters
- ☐ links
- ☐ Cuisenaire rods

- ☐ centimeter cubes
- ☐ TriOminos®
- ☐ kitty counters
- ☐ magnetic counters
- ☐ metal board
- ☐ counting chips
- ☐ milk carton tops
- ☐ Unifix™ Cubes
- ☐ base 10 blocks
- ☐ craft sticks
- ☐ Connect Four®

Environmental Materials
Learning About Money

Young children are already familiar with money. They have seen their parents and grandparents, other family members and friends use it. They need to begin their understanding of money with meaningful experiences in the classroom. Use real money periodically. At other times, use realistic replicas.

Check your room for these. If you don't have them, place a requisition next year.

Learning About Money

- ☐ magnetic coins
- ☐ money stamps
- ☐ metal board
- ☐ paper money
- ☐ money drawer
- ☐ stacking banks
- ☐ overhead coins
- ☐ stamp pads
- ☐ money
- ☐ cash register
- ☐ money clips
- ☐ spiral stacking banks

Environmental Materials
Learning About Measuring

Children will model what you do as you measure things. They will begin making comparisons and assigning their own units of measure to things. Soon they will be measuring realistically.

Check your room for these. If you don't have them, place a requisition next year.

Learning About Measuring

- ☐ rulers
- ☐ weights
- ☐ thermometers
- ☐ measuring (trundle) wheel
- ☐ funnels
- ☐ large display timer
- ☐ yardstick
- ☐ sewing measuring tape
- ☐ measuring spoons
- ☐ simple scales
- ☐ height chart
- ☐ indoor thermometer
- ☐ graduated cylinders
- ☐ barometer

- ☐ digital scales
- ☐ angle ruler
- ☐ retractable measuring tape
- ☐ measuring beakers
- ☐ balance scales
- ☐ weight chart
- ☐ outdoor thermometer
- ☐ beaker sets
- ☐ rain gauge
- ☐ analog scales
- ☐ center locator
- ☐ hem marking tape
- ☐ measuring cups
- ☐ measuring bowls

Environmental Materials
Learning to Tell Time

Young children begin understanding time as they learn to sequence things throughout the day. Posting schedules helps. Birthdays and holidays are also measured in time. The calendar begins to show children the units of days, months and years.

Check your room for these. If you don't have them, place a requisition next year.

Learning to Tell Time

- ☐ analog clock
- ☐ demonstration clock
- ☐ timers
- ☐ clock stamp
- ☐ 4" (10 cm) clock dials
- ☐ monthly calendar
- ☐ digital clock
- ☐ clock dials
- ☐ teaching clock
- ☐ blank clock sheets
- ☐ overhead clock dials
- ☐ yearly calendars

12

Environmental Materials
Learning About Geometry

Provide plenty of opportunities for children to describe, draw, sort and classify shapes of various sizes, sorts and colors.

Check your room for these. If you don't have them, place a requisition next year.

Learning About Geometry

- [ ] geometric plastic forms
- [ ] shape templates
- [ ] overhead fraction squares
- [ ] magnetic fraction squares
- [ ] magnetic fraction strips
- [ ] circle rings
- [ ] fraction tiles
- [ ] geometric foam forms
- [ ] polygon frameworks
- [ ] pattern block stamps
- [ ] fraction strips
- [ ] fraction rubber stamps
- [ ] Safe-T protractors
- [ ] fraction circles
- [ ] polygon shapes
- [ ] parquetry blocks
- [ ] overhead fraction strips
- [ ] fraction squares

Learning About Geometry

- [ ] stamp pads
- [ ] compass
- [ ] magnetic fraction circles
- [ ] tangrams
- [ ] tangram puzzles
- [ ] color tiles
- [ ] magnetic shapes
- [ ] pencils
- [ ] geoboards
- [ ] overhead tangrams
- [ ] wooden pattern blocks

- [ ] centimeter cubes
- [ ] metal board
- [ ] pens
- [ ] geoboard patterns
- [ ] tangram frames
- [ ] geometric solids
- [ ] graph paper
- [ ] paper
- [ ] markers
- [ ] geoboard bands

Children's Games Using Numbers

Games can be great teaching tools. Which ones do you have? Which ones do you want to requisition for the next buying cycle?

Number Writing

- ☐ cards
- ☐ Uno®
- ☐ Sorry®
- ☐ Parcheesi™
- ☐ Old Maid
- ☐ Crazy 8
- ☐ dominoes
- ☐ Yahtzee®
- ☐ Monopoly®
- ☐ Go Fish

Providing Math-Rich Centers

To encourage young children to use numbers, they need to be apparent in the learning environment. Provide a variety of math tools and supplies in different areas of the classroom so children will become familiar with their purpose and use.

Arts and Crafts Center

An arts and crafts center should have a variety of materials and supplies so children can create thematically related projects without much supervision; set up activities to include the use of number stencils, templates, measuring and counting at this center. It will provide a fun learning activity for your students as they learn to work independently. Which of the following materials already in your classroom or are easily available?

☐ number stamps

☐ number stencils

☐ number cards

☐ pencils and lined paper

☐ rulers

☐ compass

☐ protractor

☐ shape templates

☐ playdough

☐ clay

☐ number cookie cutters

☐ spatula, cookie sheet

Block Center

Block play centers in early childhood classrooms should contain a variety of sizes for children to use in creative construction. As your young learners engage in block activities, they will learn about geometric shapes, size, counting and comparison. Block play also provides an ideal environment for role playing as children become pilots for their airplanes, engineers for their trains and whatever else they may imagine.

Do you have these in your block area to encourage more math skills?

- ☐ shape labels for blocks
- ☐ paper of various sizes
- ☐ pencils
- ☐ crayons
- ☐ masking tape

- ☐ picture album of previously constructed structures with labels
- ☐ graph paper to draft possible constructions
- ☐ graph paper to trace block shapes onto

Dramatic Play or Housekeeping Center

A dramatic play or housekeeping area should include items such as a play sink and stove, a table and chairs, a doll bed, an ironing board, a telephone, empty cereal boxes and other grocery packages, play money and a variety of items where children will be further exposed to numbers and counting.

Bring items from home and encourage children to do so as well. Add new items regularly to add interest. Make your play center a fun and exciting learning space.

- [ ] *TV Guide*
- [ ] magazines
- [ ] daily newspapers
- [ ] number books
- [ ] recipe books or cards
- [ ] measuring spoons and cups
- [ ] catalogs
- [ ] wish list (reproducible on page 22)
- [ ] grocery list expense pad (reproducible on page 21)

- [ ] personal address book (reproducibles on pages 19 and 20)
- [ ] grocery ads
- [ ] play money
- [ ] food cans with labels
- [ ] computer or typewriter
- [ ] phone
- [ ] phone book

Address Book

_____

name

_____

address

_____

phone number

Student
photo or
personally
drawn
portrait

Address Book

_____

name

_____

address

_____

phone number

Student
photo or
personally
drawn
portrait

Address Book

_____

name

_____

address

_____

phone number

Student
photo or
personally
drawn
portrait

Address Book

_____

name

_____

address

_____

phone number

Student
photo or
personally
drawn
portrait

Address Book

_____
name

_____
address

_____
phone number

Student
photo or
personally
drawn
portrait

Address Book

_____
name

_____
address

_____
phone number

Student
photo or
personally
drawn
portrait

Address Book

_____
name

_____
address

_____
phone number

Student
photo or
personally
drawn
portrait

Address Book

_____
name

_____
address

_____
phone number

Student
photo or
personally
drawn
portrait

Grocery Expenses

Item   Cost

_____   _____

_____   _____

_____   _____

_____   _____

_____   _____

_____   _____

_____   _____

Grocery Expenses

Item   Cost

_____   _____

_____   _____

_____   _____

_____   _____

_____   _____

_____   _____

_____   _____

Grocery Expenses

Item   Cost

_____   _____

_____   _____

_____   _____

_____   _____

_____   _____

_____   _____

_____   _____

Grocery Expenses

Item   Cost

_____   _____

_____   _____

_____   _____

_____   _____

_____   _____

_____   _____

_____   _____

Wish List

Catalog	Item	Cost
___	___	___
___	___	___
___	___	___
___	___	___
___	___	___
___	___	___
___	___	___

Wish List

Catalog	Item	Cost
___	___	___
___	___	___
___	___	___
___	___	___
___	___	___
___	___	___
___	___	___

Wish List

Catalog	Item	Cost
___	___	___
___	___	___
___	___	___
___	___	___
___	___	___
___	___	___

Wish List

Catalog	Item	Cost
___	___	___
___	___	___
___	___	___
___	___	___
___	___	___
___	___	___

Reading Center

A reading center can easily accommodate math learning, too! Include a variety of the simplest board books and easy-to-read counting books. Offer a wide selection for storybooks such as "Goldilocks and the Three Bears" and other books with numbers in the title. Change books on a regular schedule so children will be eager to look for new titles.

Do you have these items?

☐ an inviting area

☐ a comfortable place to sit

☐ simple picture-number books

☐ number books to accompany your thematic unit or current project

☐ newspapers

☐ catalogs (clothing, toys, furniture)

☐ ads

☐ coupons

☐ phone books

☐ catalogs (early childhood equipment and materials)

Writing Center

Offer an assortment of interesting and easy-to-use supplies at the writing center that provides opportunities to reinforce math skills. Include pencils in different widths for beginning writers and narrow pencils for using with stencils and templates. Supply crayons and markers where children can make their own number charts or complete math worksheets.

Check to see that your center has these things, and then check to see that they have the following as well:

- ☐ simple number books
- ☐ whiteboard and markers
- ☐ chalkboards, chalk, erasers
- ☐ number stencils
- ☐ laminated numbers and shapes for tracing

- ☐ number and shape templates
- ☐ simple to complex, dot-to-dot laminated sheets
- ☐ number cards (related to unit or project)
- ☐ blank number cards to make thematic number books

Math Center

Your math center should be filled with colorful and attractive manipulatives, numbers, counters, containers, puzzles, pocket charts, pegboards, tangrams, parquetry blocks, magnetic boards, clocks, dice, beads and a calculator. Include games that focus on beginning math skills such as dominoes and bingo.

Check your math center for these items:

- [ ] paper of various sizes, shapes and colors
- [ ] pencils of various sizes and colors
- [ ] number and counting books
- [ ] number, word, object charts
- [ ] written problem-solving strips
- [ ] calendar pocket chart with month and days of the week

- [ ] number-word cards
- [ ] grocery ads and grocery lists
- [ ] catalogs
- [ ] dominoes
- [ ] bingo
- [ ] Go Fish!

Charts and Signs

So much goes on in an early child-hood room. Provide plenty of visually appealing items that will encourage your children to count.

Make or use charts and signs for each of the following:

- ☐ calendars
- ☐ weather charts
- ☐ attendance charts—How many children are present? How many children are absent?
- ☐ maps
- ☐ health pyramid (Count and record your snack and meal.)
- ☐ number charts (1-10, 1-20, 1-10) (pages 27 to 29)
- ☐ lunch charts—How many children brought lunch to school? How many children will buy lunch?

26

1

2

3

4

5

6

7

8

9

10

1	11
2	12
3	13
4	14
5	15
6	16
7	17
8	18
9	19
10	20

1	11	21	31	41	51	61	71	81	91
2	12	22	32	42	52	62	72	82	92
3	13	23	33	43	53	63	73	83	93
4	14	24	34	44	54	64	74	84	94
5	15	25	35	45	55	65	75	85	95
6	16	26	36	46	56	66	76	86	96
7	17	27	37	47	57	67	77	87	97
8	18	28	38	48	58	68	78	88	98
9	19	29	39	49	59	69	79	89	99
10	20	30	40	50	60	70	80	90	100

Science Center

Young children love to investigate creepy crawlies and watch seeds grow into plants. Stock your science center with ladybug and ant farms, plant-growing activities and magnifying glasses for students to observe small changes. Include progress charts to show dates when seeds were planted and first sprouted. Measure the plants as they grow. Use measuring cups to add water. Add new items from your district science center and local nurseries for continuing interest.

Check your science center for these items:

☐ variety of shapes, sizes and colors of paper

☐ variety of colors and sizes of markers and pencils

☐ recording sheets for experiments

☐ science recording journals

☐ life science books

☐ life cycle charts

☐ thermometer

☐ weather charts

☐ labels on each item

☐ science counting books

☐ growth charts

☐ scales

☐ rulers

NUMBERS, NUMBER WORDS AND SETS

Included on the next several pages are number strips that contain the number, the number word and a set of objects to match the number. The objects are only dots on these pages so that you may use them with any unit of study.

The sets presented here are visually positioned to look at in groups of five or 10. For example, 7 is a group of 5 and 2 more. Twelve is a group of 10 (2 fives) and 2 more. Once students have mastered these, provide other visual settings. For example, 7 as a group of six and one more; 12 is two groups of six; etc.

Purchase sets of small stickers. Place stickers over the dots to match themes of study. Or have the children place the stickers over the dots as they count the numbers.

Post strips in the room from 0-10 in one column and 11-20 in the next column. This will set up base 10 charts that students can use later.

	•	• •
zero	one	two
0	1	2

•••	••••	•••••
three	four	five
3	4	5

● ● ● ● ● ●	● ● ● ● ● ● ●	● ● ● ● ● ● ● ●
six	seven	eight
6	7	8

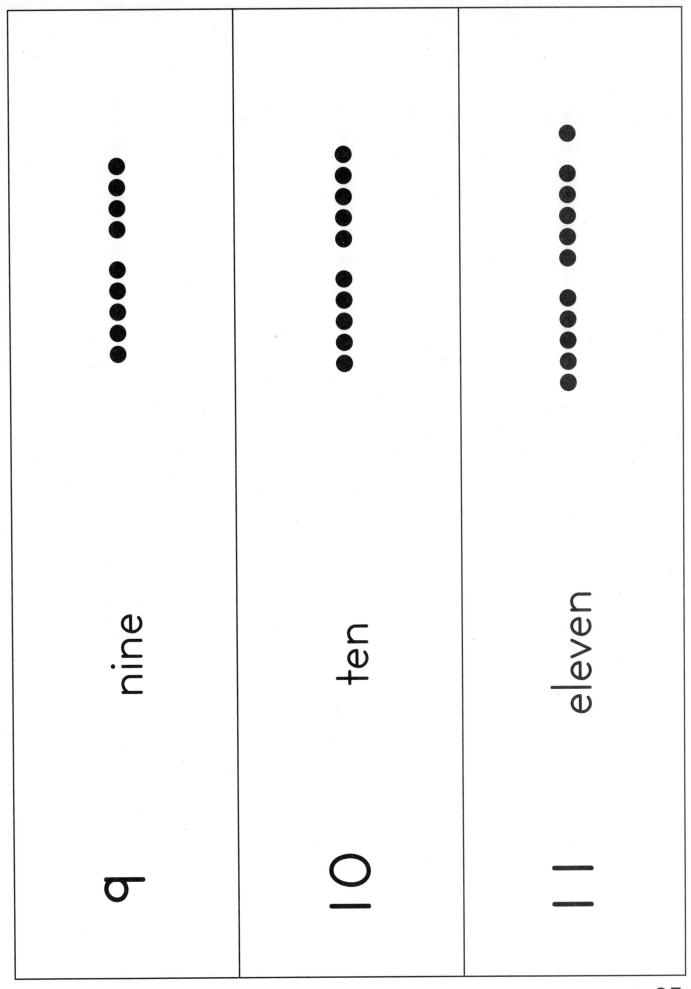

nine

9

ten

10

eleven

11

• • • • • • • • • • • •	• • • • • • • • • • • • •	• • • • • • • • • • • • • •
twelve	thirteen	fourteen
12	13	14

15 fifteen	16 sixteen	17 seventeen

eighteen	nineteen	twenty
18	19	20

Number Boards

Use the number and set in the box on the right to place on cards. There are several sets to match various units on pages 45 to 58. Make a number board with 20 pockets— one pocket per number from 1-20. For each unit of study, make number cards using stickers to match the unit. Place the appropriate number of stickers at one end of the card and the number upside down at the opposite end so that either will show when one end is in the pocket.

For more advanced students, put the number at one end and the number word upside down at the opposite end.

1 one

Number Stickies

Cut out the number-set box on pages 32-38. Paste it at the top of a half sheet of poster board, laminate and post in the classroom. Have children glue on pictures, stickers or draw things on sticky notes to display on the chart.

EXPLORING NUMBERS

Number-Set Cards

Cut out the number box and the picture box together. Fold in half. Stand the number-picture cards up on a table with one child on each side of the card. One child reads the number and the other counts the number in the set.

Chalkboard Number Train

Cut out each of the number cards (pages 32–38) and enlarge for bulletin board use. Glue wheels on to each to make a train boxcar. Design an engine from black paper. Laminate the set. Make a number train to hang from the chalk tray in the room.

Countertop Number Boxcars

Glue each of the pictures onto small boxes or milk cartons covered with construction paper. Place them on a countertop in the classroom and have children count objects to put in the boxes that show their understanding of the number.

40

Using Number Pages

Number pages can be used in a variety of ways to enhance math skills in your classroom. Children can easily construct their own pages after you demonstrate and make a sample of each different one.

Listed below—in sequential order of difficulty—are a variety of ways these pages can be used. Assign pages to children according to their individual levels.

Number Page Activities

Sponge Stamps

Cut out numbers from sponges. Pour thick tempera paints into plastic plates. Children dip sponge number into paint and apply several times randomly to a piece of paper. Allow to dry. Send paper home to be used as wrapping paper. Children return to school with a number of objects wrapped in the paper. Display items on unfolded paper with sponge numbers showing.

Number Stamps

Use number stamps to match numbers on a page.

Instant Pudding

Laminate paper. Cover activity area with newsprint or other protective covering. Prepare any flavor instant pudding and spread onto piece of paper. Children practice writing numbers in the pudding. Use a spatula to smooth out pudding for another child to use.

Pasta Numbers

Use small dry pasta shapes and glue to form numbers in the center of the page and glue to the paper.

Many Times, Many Colors

Write the number several times on the page using a variety of media: pencils, colored pencils, crayons, watercolors, markers, colored glue, etc.

Space Station

Have students use space markers to stamp the entire page of one item. Circle the right number of objects with string or yarn glued onto the paper.

Unit Blocks

Provide children with unit blocks. Have them count the corresponding number of blocks to place on the paper.

Big Numbers from Small Numbers

Form a large number by using several smaller numbers.

EXPLORING NUMBERS

Number Cut-Outs

Cut out numbers from magazines, catalogs or newspapers and glue them onto the page with the corresponding number.

Number Rainbow

Make a rainbow using each number. Form a number using red, orange, yellow, green, blue and purple.

Number Patterns

Practice writing the numbers with various colors to form patterns.

Sparkly or Sandy Numbers

Write a large number in the center of the page. Cover it with glue. Sprinkle glitter on the number. Children trace around the glittery number.

EXPLORING NUMBERS

Sets of Objects

Locate pictures that have sets of objects or groups of people in them. Cut out and glue onto the number sheet.

Friends

Find a friend in the room, in your family, in your school or in a story who is your same age. Find others who are different ages. Write the friends' names on the appropriate number page.

Numbers and Sizes

Divide a piece of paper in half. Label one half *smaller* and the other half *larger*. Place a number at the top. Children find two sets of corresponding number objects and place them in the correct half.

Handwriting

Provide a large number sample on lined paper. Children practice writing the number and/or number word several times. Circle the best one.

Scavenger Hunt

Give each child a small paper bag and piece of paper with a number from 1 – 10 on it. Go on an outdoor scavenger hunt to find a set of similar items to match the number. Glue items onto paper and display with descriptive labels: *two pebbles, three leaves, four broken twigs.*

Noticing Numbers

Have children cut out two-digit numbers from newspapers and catalogs. Glue onto appropriate number page according to first digit. For example: glue numbers 20–29 on page number 2.

44

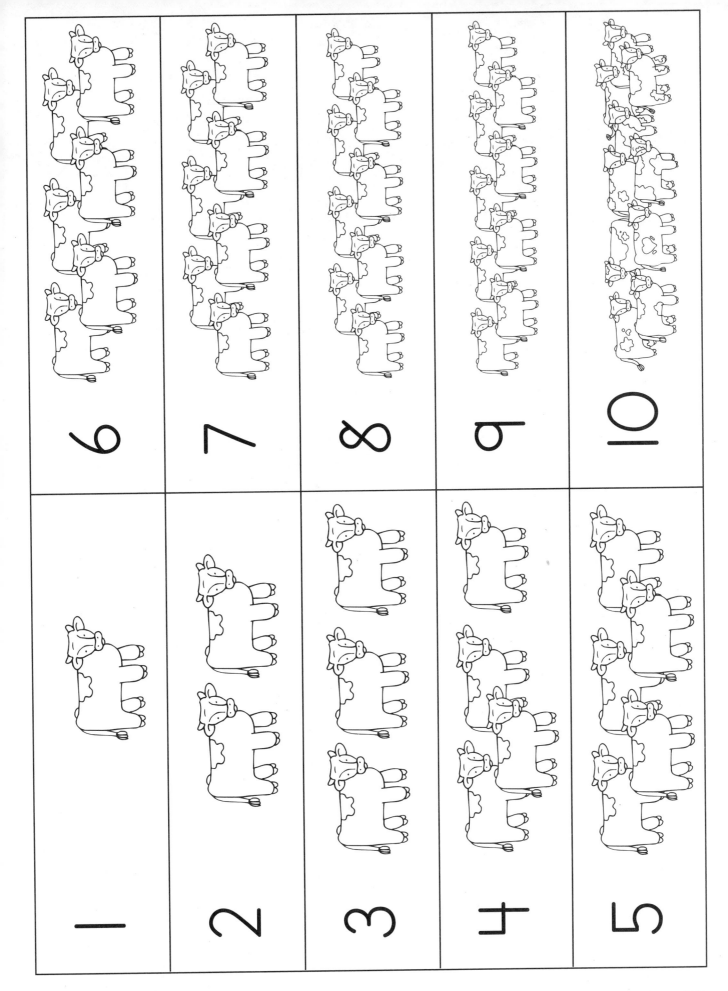

6   7   8   9   10

1   2   3   4   5

NUMBERS FOR UNITS

Visit the school and neighborhood libraries. Select several fiction and nonfiction books about cows. Read them to the children and retell the stories using flannel board cut-outs and puppets. Some charming books include:

Jackson, Woody. *Counting Cows.* San Diego: Harcourt Brace & Co., 1995.

Cows

Counting 10 Cows

Use the 10 cow cards on page 45. Have children put together two cards to make a cow set of 10. Write an addition sentence for each different set. How many ways can children make sets of 10? (Note: 1 + 9 and 9 + 1 are considered different ways.)

Photo Hunt

Go on a hunt in magazines for pictures with milk mustaches. How many can you find?

Milk Products

Have each child name and draw a picture of a different product that is made from milk. Place on a large cow-shaped piece of white paper. Count them.

Heads, Legs and Tails

How many heads do 10 cows have?

How many legs do 10 cows have?

How many tails do 10 cows have?

What about the eyes, nose and hooves?

46

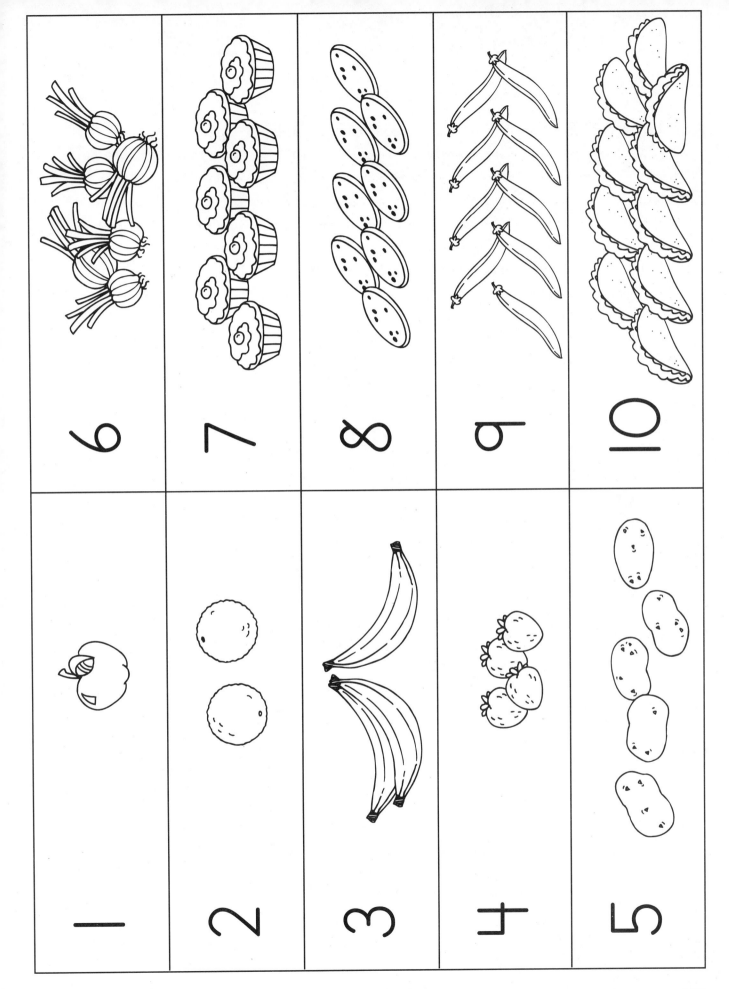

6

7

8

9

10

1

2

3

4

5

NUMBERS FOR UNITS

Foods

Gather several books about foods. Some popular titles include:

Carle, Eric. *The Very Hungry Caterpillar* (available in many languages). New York: Philomel Books, 1994.

Giganti, Paul. *Each Orange Had 8 Slices: A Counting Book*. New York: Greenwillow Books, 1992.

Hutchins, Pat. *The Doorbell Rang*. New York: Greenwillow Books, 1989.

McGrath, Barbara Barbieri. *The m & m's Counting Book*. Watertown, MA: Charlesbridge, Pub., 1994.

McMillan, Bruce. *Eating Fractions*. New York: Scholastic, 1992.

McMillan, Bruce. *Jelly Beans for Sale*. New York: Scholastic, 1996.

Stevens, Janet. *Tops and Bottoms*. San Diego: Harcourt Brace, 1995.

Tofts, Hannah. *I Eat Fruit!* New York: Larousse Kingfisher Chambers, 1998.

Tofts, Hannah. *I Eat Vegetables!* New York: Larousse Kingfisher Chambers, 1998.

Retell the stories using pictures of food mounted on poster board and made into small finger puppets.

Food

The Other Half

Select 2 oranges, 2 apples, 2 bananas, 2 potatoes and 2 heads of cabbage. Cut each in half. Give one to each of 20 children. Can they find their other half? Once they put all their halves together, how many wholes do they have?

The Hungry Caterpillar

Retell *The Very Hungry Caterpillar* using foods from one of the food groups, then the others. Try using candy bars. Let children illustrate the story.

How Much Does It Weigh?

Weigh several foods and record the weight of each.

Count m & m's®

Sort and count m & m's®. Which color has the most m & m's®? Which color has the least m & m's®? How many m & m's® are there if you add all the red and green together? How many m & m's® are there if you add all the yellow together? How many m & m's® are there if you add all the yellow and brown together?

6	7	8	9	10

1	2	3	4	5

Rabbits

Collect bunny and rabbit books. Retell the stories using finger puppets made from cotton balls.

Baker, Alan. *Brown Rabbit's Shape Book.* New York: Kingfisher Books, 1994.

Baker, Alan. *Gray Rabbit's 1, 2, 3.* New York: Kingfisher Books, 1994.

Brown, Margaret Wise. *The Runaway Bunny.* New York: HarperCollins. 1985.

Grossman, Virginia. *Ten Little Rabbits.* San Francisco: Chronicle Books, 1998.

Kunhardt, Dorothy. *Pat the Bunny.* Golden/Western, 1987.

Mathews, Louise. *Bunches & Bunches of Bunnies,* 1990.

Wane, Heather. *10 Little Bunnies,* New York: Golden Books, 1998.

Rabbits

Sorting

Make a set of cut-out bunny shapes of different sizes from colored poster board. Let children sort them according to size and color.

Counting

Make bunnies out of cotton balls, wiggly eyes and two pink construction paper ears. Attach a magnet to the back of each. Cut out the number cards on page 49. Place a magnetic strip on the back of each. Place the materials next to the filing cabinet. Have children put up the 1 card and one cotton bunny.

Left-Right Bunnies

Cut out bunnies from white and brown construction paper, and line up along chalkboard ledge. Which ones are facing right? Which ones are facing left?

Measure Them

Invite children to bring stuffed bunnies from home. Measure the ears, legs and bodies. Which one is the shortest? Which one is the longest?

6

7

8

9

10

1

2

3

4

5

NUMBERS FOR UNITS

Puppies

Read several books about dogs, puppies and counting. Retell the stories using puppy cut-outs. Try these:

Moore, Elaine. *Roly Poly Puppies.* New York: Cartwheel Books, 1996.

Nelson, Jo Anne. *Ten Little Puppies.* Los Angeles: Price Stern Sloan, 1989.

Nelson, Jo Anne. *Ten Little Puppies* (audiocassette). Los Angeles, CA: Price Stern Sloan, 1989.

Singer, Muff. *Puppy Says 1, 2, 3.* New York: Random House, 1993.

Stoeke, Janet M. *One Little Puppy Dog.* New York: Dutton, 1998.

Puppies

Sorting

Have children cut out photographs of dogs from magazines and catalogs. Glue onto pieces of poster board. Sort according to the sizes of the dogs.

Puppy Puppets

Use brown lunch bags to make puppets. Add construction paper features. Write a large number from 1–10 on the front of each puppet. Children make their puppet jump, lie down or bark that many times.

Shape Puppies

Use rectangles and circles of various sizes to form puppies.

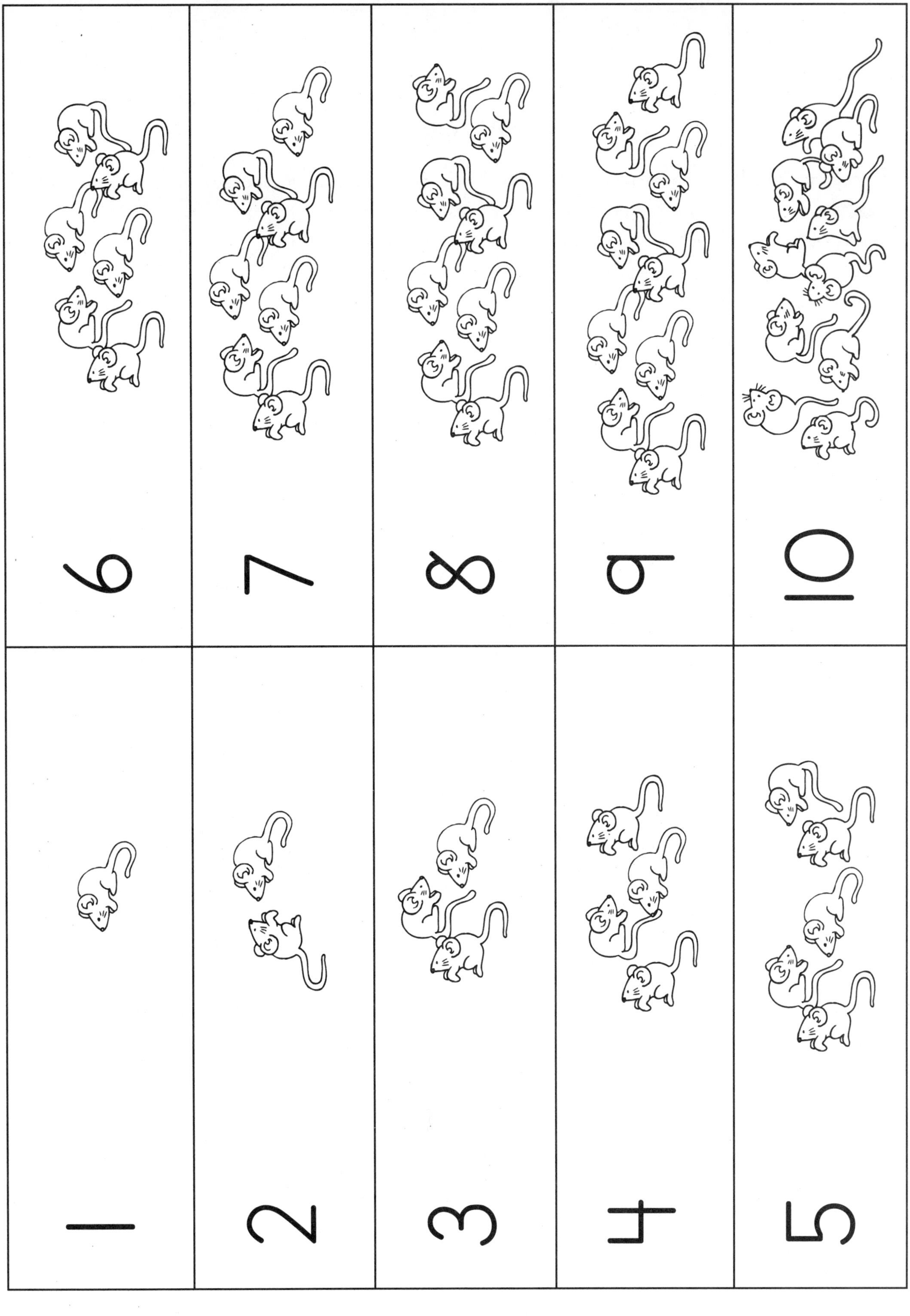

6

7

8

9

10

1

2

3

4

5

NUMBERS FOR UNITS

Mice

Encourage children to contribute to this class collection and bring in books about mice. In addition, read and display some of the following titles:

Baker, Alan. *Two Tiny Mice*. New York: Dial Books for Young Readers, 1991.

Cousins, Lucy. *Count with Maisy*. Cambridge, MA: Candlewick Press, 1997.

Dunbar, Joyce. *Ten Little Mice*. San Diego: Harcourt Brace Jovanovich, 1995.

Walsh, Ellen. *Mouse Count*. San Diego: Harcourt Brace, 1995.

Young, Ed. *Seven Blind Mice*. New York: Philomel Books, 1992.

Mice

10 Facts About Mice

Read about mice in the encyclopedia, in a book or on a CD-ROM. Make a list of 10 facts about mice.

Investigate

Which is longer, the mouse or the tail? The mouse or the nose? The mouse or the ear? The mouse or the ?

Count the Eyes, Noses and Feet

Use one number card from page 53 and the graph on page 105. Write the number of mice from 1-10 horizontally across the bottom. Draw illustrations of eyes, nose, tail and feet vertically along the left side. Count and record the number of each feature to match the mouse number card. Try this activity orally. How many tails will seven mice have? How many eyes are there on three mice? How many noses on six mice?

In Order 1-10

Make cards from the mice numbers on page 53. Put the numbers in order, 1-10.

6

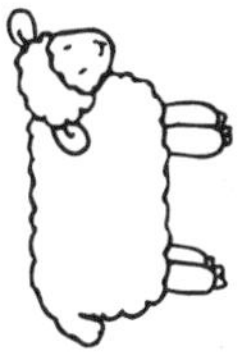

7

8

9

10

1

2

3

4

5

Sheep

Sheep appear frequently in popular bedtime stories. Choose several books where children learn about sheep as they reinforce counting skills.

Bang, Molly. *Ten, Nine, Eight*. New York: Tupelo Books, 1998.

Enderle, Judith. *Six Creepy Sheep*. Honesdale, PA: Caroline House, Boyds Mills Press, 1992.

Keller, Holly. *Ten Sleepy Sheep*. New York: Greenwillow Books, 1983.

Sheep

Counting Backwards

Read Molly Bang's *Ten, Nine, Eight*. Reread it saying the numbers backwards. Line up 10 children in your room and count forward and backward.

10 Sleepy Sheep

Make 10 sheep from poster board. Glue on cotton balls. Use clothespins in the front and back for legs. Use the 10 sheep to retell the story.

Fill the Bags

Teach the nursery rhyme Baa Baa Black Sheep. Fill plastic zip-top bags with yarn. Repeat the rhyme with varying numbers of bags full. Whom are the bags of yarn for?

My Sheep, Your Sheep

Invite the children to bring in stuffed lambs and sheep from home. Sort them according to size.

Jump over the Fence

Tape masking tape to the playground surface or use chalk to make 10 fences. Play follow the leader and jump 10 fences, counting each one as the jump is made.

1	6
2	7
3	8
4	9
5	10

NUMBERS FOR UNITS

Frogs and Insects

Children's fascination with insects will spark their interest in stories about all sorts of insects and frogs as well. Read some of these suggested titles, and look for other books that feature counting and numbers as a theme.

Carle, Eric. *The Very Hungry Caterpillar*. New York: Philomel Books, 1994.

Hooker, Yvonne. *One Green Frog*. New York: Grosset and Dunlop, 1989.

Pinczes, Elinor. *One Hundred Hungry Ants*. Boston: Houghton Mifflin, 1993.

Souza, Dorothy M. *Eight Legs*. Minneapolis: Carolrhoda Books, 1991.

Sturges, Philemon. *Ten Flashing Fireflies*. New York: North-South Books, 1997.

Frogs and Insects

The Very Hungry Frog

Retell the story *The Very Hungry Caterpillar*, this time having the frog eating insects. What happens to the frog in the end?

Counting Legs

How many legs does each have?

a person	two people
a frog	three frogs
an insect	two insects
a spider	two spiders

How many legs does a chair have? Two chairs?

Do other things have the same number of legs?

10 Flashing Fireflies

Give 10 flashlights to 10 children. Darken the room. Have everyone close their eyes. Say "10 flashing fireflies" which is the signal to flash the lights. Look up to the ceiling. Where are the lights? Count them.

Frogs on a Log

Make celery strips with peanut butter. Add raisins for frogs. Count the number of frogs on each log and eat.

MAKING NUMBER BOOKS

After reading aloud several attractive and colorful children's books featuring numbers, shapes, clocks and items to count, demonstrate how children can make their own number book using blank books of stapled pages, spiral-bound notebooks or 4" x 6" (10" x 15" cm) index cards. As a large group cooperative activity, make a class math board book using matte board and binder rings.

Making Blank Number Books

Fold three sheets of paper in half to form a book of numbers from 1-10. Staple three times at the center fold. Use the front page as the title page. Children start with number 1 on the inside left page and write each number from 2-10 on succeeding pages using both left and right pages. Punch holes in upper left corner and connect cards in numerical order with yarn.

Number Book Activities

Working with any of the above formats, use the following activities to complete number books based on individual students' needs.

1. Write a number from 1-10 on each page. Children draw or cut out the corresponding number of objects to paste on each page.

2. Paste a variety of pictures showing squares, triangles, circles, rectangles onto separate pages.

3. Cut and paste individual pages of 1s, 2s, 3s, etc., in different sizes from magazines, catalogs and newspapers.

4. Write each number word on a page. Children draw a set of objects to match each number.

MAKING NUMBER BOOKS

Class Board Books

To make a board book, ask your local frame shop for 13 scrap matte boards cut into approximately 5" x 5" (13 x 13 cm) squares. Bright colors will provide attractive backgrounds for each page of numbers and pictures. Set aside three boards to be used for the front and back covers and title page. Paste a number word and corresponding number to the top of each of 10 boards. Invite children to cut and paste objects onto each board to match the number. Drill holes on the left side of each board and put pages in sequence with binder rings.

As a small group activity, assign children to work cooperatively as they bring pictures from home, glue and label the pages. Assign different themes or subjects to each group such as foods, animals, insects.

Using Math Board Books

Working with any of the previous formats, use the following activities to complete number books based on individual students' needs.

1. Make a display of the completed number books.

2. Encourage children to read one another's books.

3. Use books to read to the class as a whole.

4. Invite parents, and then have children read and show their completed books.

24

twenty-four

1

one

23

twenty-three

2

two

22

twenty-two

3

three

21

twenty-one

4

four

Math Books

20

twenty

5

five

Math Books

19

nineteen

6

six

18

eighteen

7

seven

17

seventeen

8

eight

Math Books

16

sixteen

9

nine

15
fifteen

10
ten

14

fourteen

11

eleven

13

thirteen

12

twelve

Math Books

SHOPPING LISTS

Search and Cut

Have children look for numbers in simple search and cut activities. Provide catalogs, newspaper grocery inserts and magazines. Direct children to cut out items they would like to buy along with the corresponding prices. Glue onto page for individual pictorial shopping list.

Advanced learners can cut items and sort into categories such as fruits and vegetables, meat, cereals, dairy, canned goods and other familiar supermarket sections. Glue each category of pictures onto a separate page and staple together to make a supermarket shopping booklet.

SHOPPING LISTS

What to Buy

Have children search the grocery ads in the local newspaper to choose three, four and five things that their parents frequently buy. Children copy the items and prices from the paper to take home to their parents.

Most Expensive? Least Expensive?

Use a calculator to add up prices of two, three and four items. Repeat, selecting other items. Which group of products costs the most? Which group of items costs the least? Use comparative words such as *most, least, more than, less than.*

Add up the costs of each child's list. Arrange in order from the least expensive shopping list to the the most expensive. Mix up shopping lists and see if any children can put them back in order.

74

_____'s

Supermarket Shopping Booklet

Look for items in the newspaper or in catalogs you might like to have. Cut out and glue onto this sheet.

_____'s

Shopping List

Look for items in the newspaper or in catalogs you might like to have. Cut out and glue onto this sheet.

1 Things That Stand Alone

Explain to children that some things stand alone. There is only one. Show the illustrations below—there is only one sun; there is only one moon. Ask children to think about their bodies. What do they have only one of? (one nose but two nostrils, one mouth but two lips, one neck, one head, one belly button) What other things can children name that there is only one of? Guide discussion to ideas such as: our school has one principal, one cafeteria, one library.

Name _____   Date _____

Look at the pictures below that stand alone.

How many others can you think of?

|

|

2 Things That Come in Pairs or in Twos

Explain to children that many things come in pairs. Show the illustrations below—sleeves, pant legs, mittens and boots come in pairs. What parts of our bodies do we have two of? Guide discussion to include shoulders, elbows, wrists, knees, cheeks, thumbs. Ask children what items their parents buy that come in pairs.

Name _____   Date _____

How many others can you think of?

Are there any in our room?

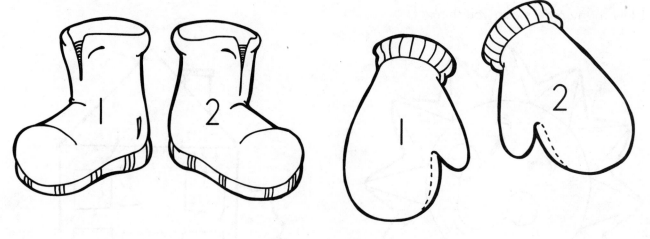

3   Things That Come in Threes

Name _____   Date _____

Some things come in threes.

Look at the pictures below.

How many others can you think of?

Are there any in our room?

4   Things That Come in Fours

Name _____   Date _____

Many things come in fours.

Look at the pictures below that come in fours.

How many others can you think of?

Are there any in our room?

5   Things That Come in Fives

Name _____   Date _____

Many things come in fives.

Look at the pictures below that come in fives.

How many others can you think of?

Are there any in our room?

6   Things That Come in Sixes

Name _____   Date _____

Some things come in sixes.

Look at the pictures below that come in sixes.

How many others can you think of?

Are there any in our room?

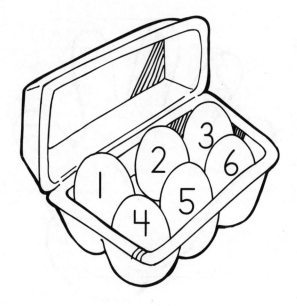

Things That Stick Together in Numbers

Name _____   Date _____

Many things come in pairs. Some things stand alone.

Some come in threes, fours, fives, sixes and twelves—or dozens.

Beside each number word below, list things found in that amount. A few samples are done for you. Let the children be creative in their thinking!

ones _____ _____ _____

twos _____ eyes _____ _____ _____

threes _____ _____ _____

fours _____ _____ _____

fives ___ basketball team __ _____ _____

sixes _____ _____ _____

sevens _____ _____ _____

eights _____ _____ _____

nines _____ _____ _____

tens __ pennies in a dime __ _____ _____

dozen _____ eggs _____ _____ _____

Create separate charts to show things that come in ones and things that come in twos, threes and fours. Encourage children to bring in pictures and paste them onto the appropriate chart.

Ask questions to see who can answer the fastest. How many wheels are on a car? How many legs does a bird have? How many fingers in a glove? How many stems on a pumpkin? How many tails on a mouse? How many legs on a giraffe? How many skates in a pair? How many colors on a flag?

CLIP AND COPY
MEASURES AND ACTIVITIES

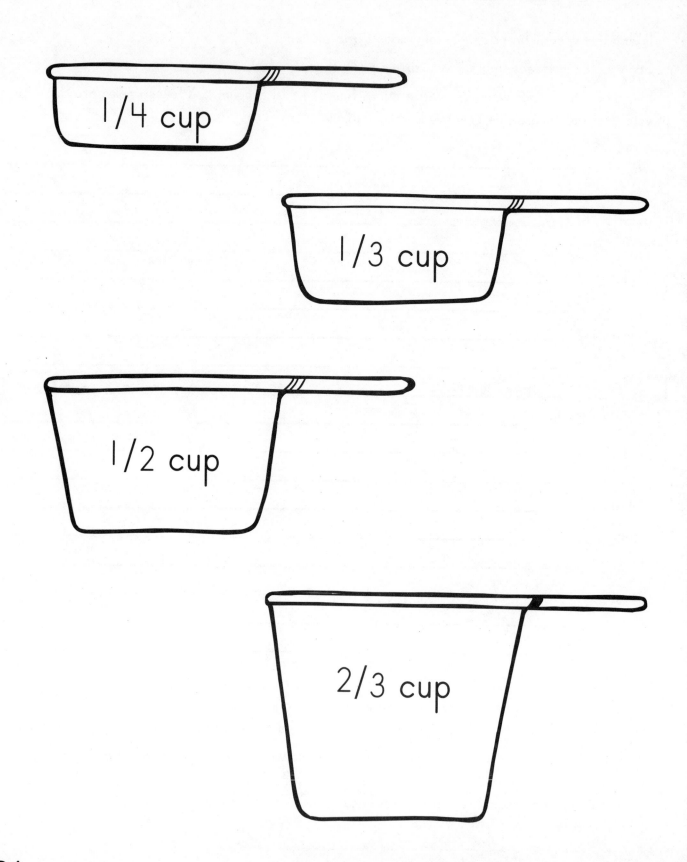

1/4 cup

1/3 cup

1/2 cup

2/3 cup

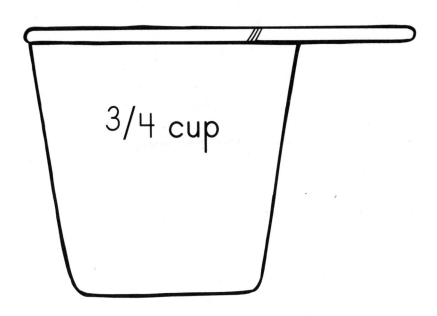

3/4 cup

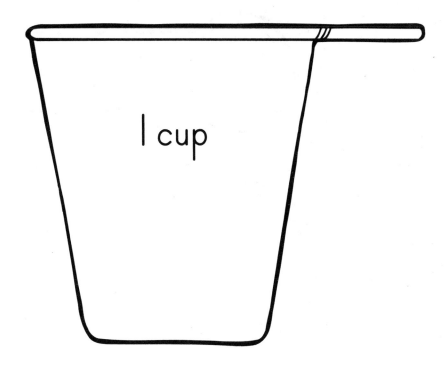

I cup

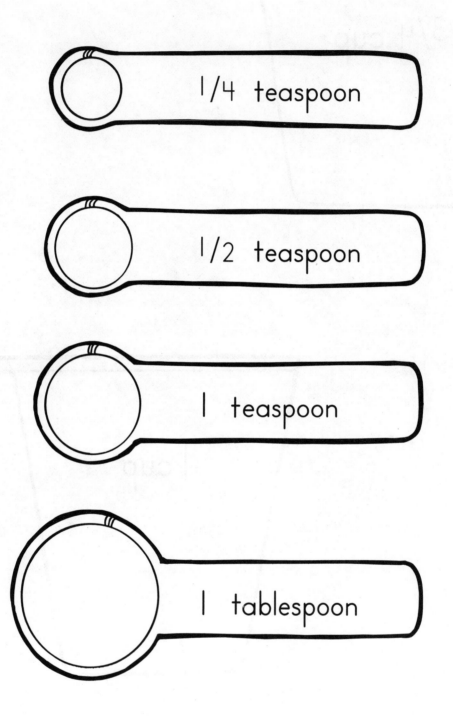

1/4 teaspoon

1/2 teaspoon

1 teaspoon

1 tablespoon

TLC10191 Copyright © Teaching & Learning Company, Carthage, IL 62321-0010

CLIP AND COPY
MEASURES AND ACTIVITIES

Resources

Use the following resources to prepare fun recipes and teach measuring skills.

Knox, G. M. *Cookies for Kids*. Des Moines, IA: Meredith Corporation, 1983.

Recipes

Make "Number Pretzels" and "Nutty Numbers" as described in Kinder Krunchies.

Number Pretzels (Jenkins)

Dissolve:	1 T. (15 ml) yeast in
	1/2 c. (120 ml) warm water
Add:	1 t. (5 ml) honey
	1 t. (5 ml) salt
Add:	1 1/3 c. (320 ml) flour

Knead.

Roll pieces on waxed paper.

Form numbers.

Nutty Numbers (Jenkins)

Mix	1/2 c. (120 ml) soft butter
	1 c. (240 ml) flour
	1/4 c. (60 ml) honey
	1 c. (240 ml) wheat germ
	Shape into numbers.

Cover with chopped nuts.

Press gently.

Bake at 350°F (177°C) for 10 minutes.

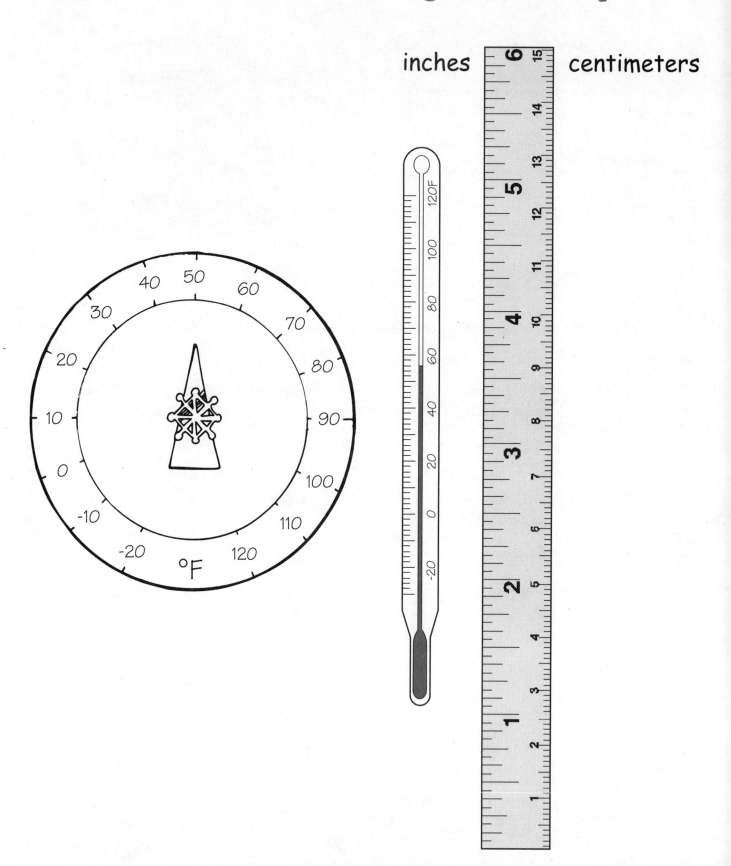

inches   centimeters

CLIP AND COPY
MEASURES AND ACTIVITIES

Resources

Allen, Pamela. *Who Sank the Boat?* New York: Paper Star, 1996.

Pluckrose, Henry. *Mouth Counts Series: Length*. Chicago: Children's Press, 1995.

Pluckrose, Henry. *Mouth Counts Series: Size*. Chicago: Children's Press, 1995.

Try these activities:

- ☐ measure one another
- ☐ measure your shoe
- ☐ measure your sleeve
- ☐ measure your pinky
- ☐ measure a book
- ☐ measure a crayon
- ☐ measure the tabletop
- ☐ measure floor tile
- ☐ measure your friend's nose
- ☐ measure your big toe
- ☐ measure a pencil
- ☐ measure a marker

What else can you measure?

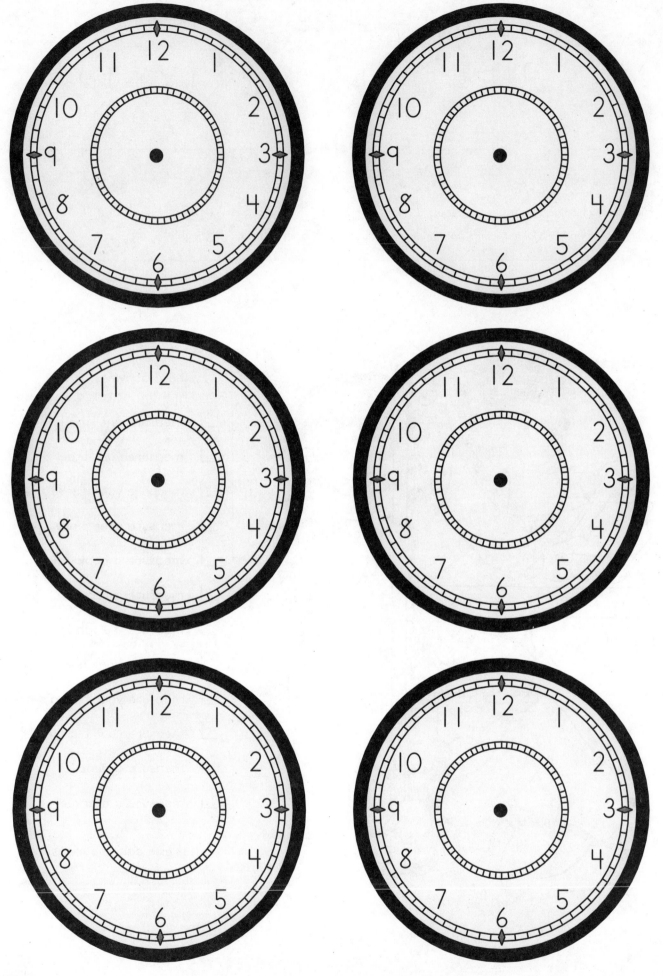

What time is it when . . . ?

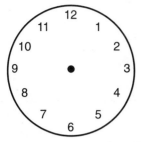

you come to school?

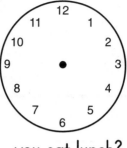

you eat lunch?

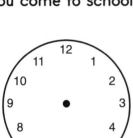

you have a snack?

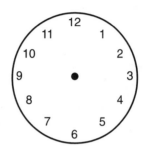

you go outside?

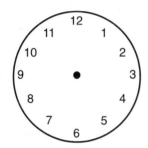

you go home?

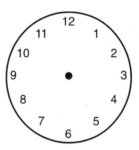

you go to bed?

Share these timely stories about time and then place in the reading or math center for children to read independently or with a friend.

Anastasio, Dina. *It's About Time*. New York: Grosset & Dunlop, Inc., 1993.

Bang, Molly. *Ten, Nine, Eight*. New York: Tupelo Books, 1998.

Carle, Eric. *The Grouchy Ladybug*. New York: HarperCollins Juvenile Books, 1996.

Carle, Eric. *The Very Hungry Caterpillar*. New York: Philomel Books, 1991.

Carle, Eric. *Today Is Monday*. New York: Paper Star, 1997.

Chambless, R. *The Real Mother Goose Clock Book*. New York: Cartwheel Books, 1994.

Inkpen, Mick. *One Bear at Bedtime: A Counting Book*. Boston: Little, Brown, 1992.

Keller, Holly. *Ten Sleepy Sheep*. New York: Greenwillow Books, 1983.

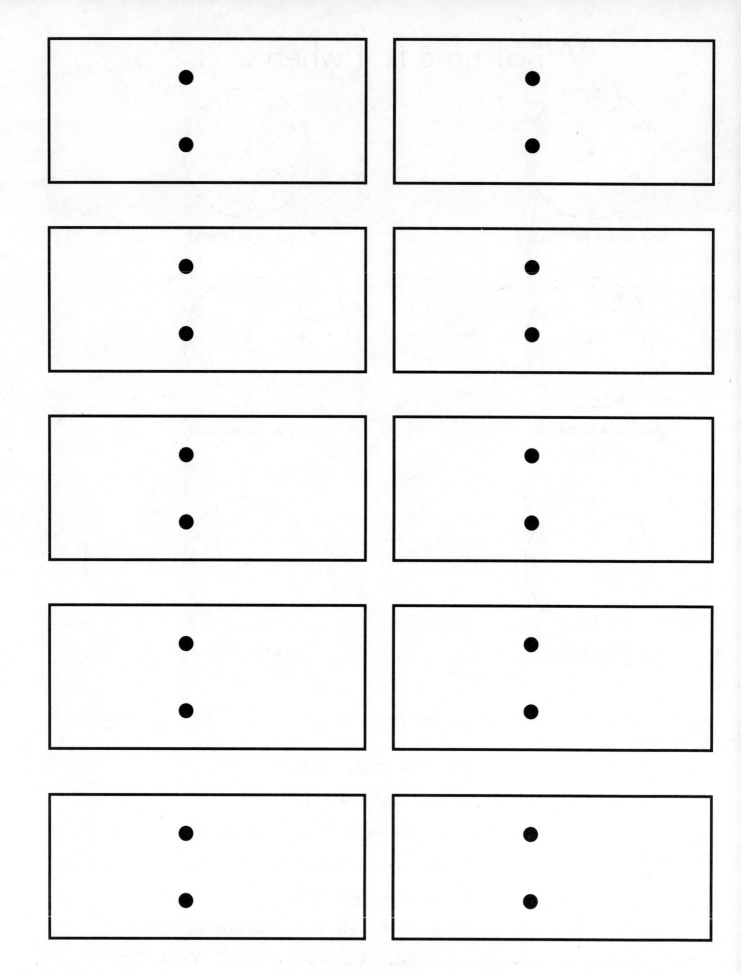

What time is it when . . . ?

:
you come to school?

:
you eat lunch?

:
you have a snack?

:
you go outside?

:
you go home?

:
you go to bed?

Timer

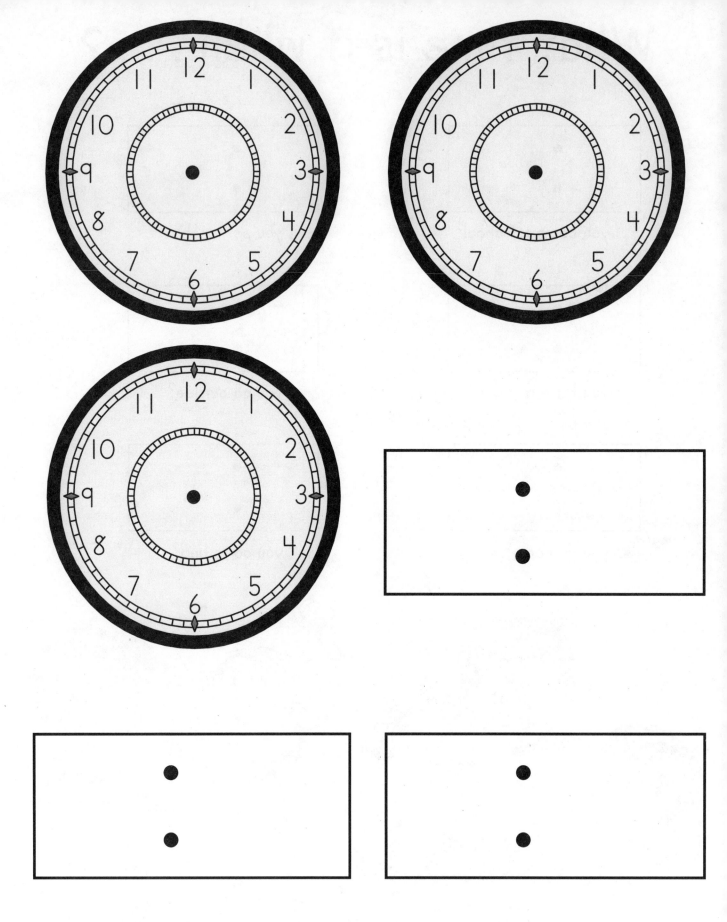

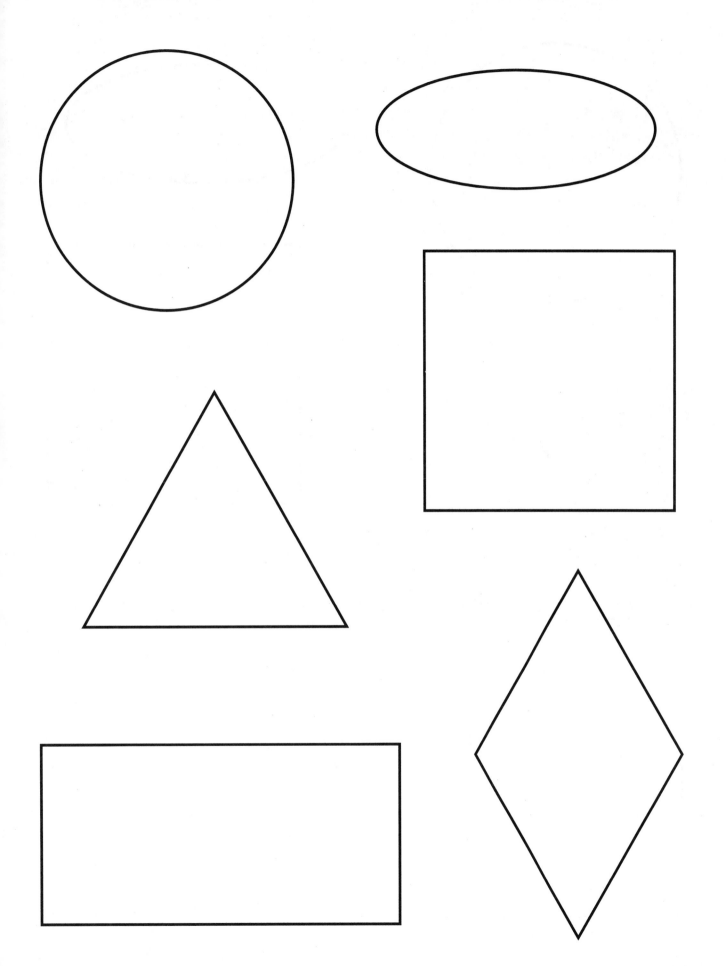

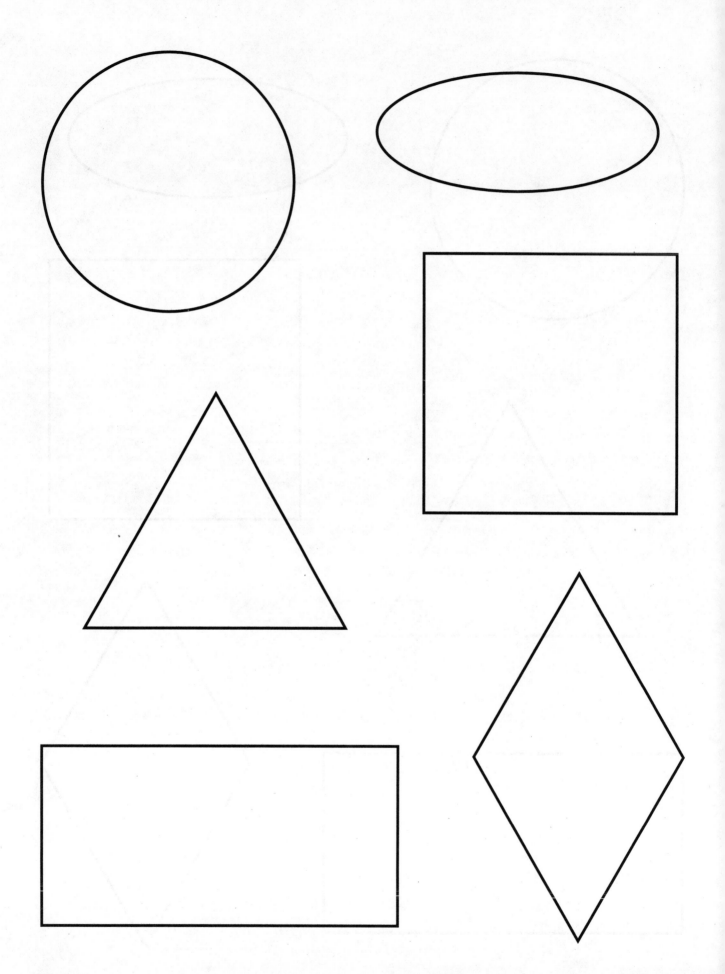

96

CLIP AND COPY
MEASURES AND ACTIVITIES

Resources

Everything has a shape! Set up a colorful display of books about shapes including these titles:

Dodds, Dayle Ann. *The Shape of Things*. Cambridge, MA: Candlewick Press, 1996.

Ehlert, Lois. *Color Train*. New York: Lippincott, 1990.

Ehlert, Lois. *Color Zoo*. New York: HarperCollins Juvenile Books, 1997.

Hoban, Tana. *Shapes, Shapes, Shapes*. New York: Mulberry Books, 1996.

MacCarone, Grace. *The Silly Story of Goldie Locks and the Three Squares*. New York: Cartwheel Books, 1996.

McMillan, Bruce. *Eating Fractions*. New York: Scholastic, 1992.

Pluckrose, Henry. *Mouth Counts Series: Shape*. Chicago: Children's Press, 1995.

Voss, Gi. *Museum Shapes*. Boston: Boston Museum of Fine Arts, 1994.

Shape Activities

Shape Cookies

Use shape cookie cutters to make shape cookies from already prepared sugar dough.

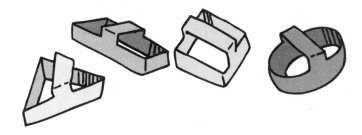

Food Shapes

Ask children to bring in different-shaped food samples from home—square crackers, round cookies, an oval hard-boiled egg, etc. Serve foods of several shapes for children to enjoy. Cut fresh pineapple into wedges for a triangular shape. Spread cream cheese on rectangular melba toast crackers. Cut slices of bread spread with peanut butter and jelly into four squares. Serve round mini rice cakes.

Shape Search

Read *Museum Shapes* (Voss). Then give each child a different shape. Ask children to locate items in the room of the same shape. Vary the shapes of rectangles and triangles, and the sizes of circles, squares and ovals.

CLIP AND COPY
MEASURES AND ACTIVITIES

Paper Shapes

Provide shape templates for children to practice tracing a variety of shapes. After tracing outlines, go over lines with crayons or markers.

Shape Search

Read *Museum Shapes* (Voss). Then give each child a different shape. Ask children to locate items in the room of the same shape. Vary the shapes of rectangles and triangles, and the sizes of circles, squares, and ovals.

Painted Circles

Have children trace a variety of large circular items onto butcher paper. Go over the borders with a brush and tempera paint to show bold outlines of different-sized circles.

What's the Shape?

Place tangram pieces or similar assorted shapes into a paper bag. Have children close their eyes, reach in and remove one shape. Without opening their eyes, can they identify the shape?

10 pennies

1 dime

2 nickels

one dollar bill

2 half dollars

4 quarters

five dollar bill

ten dollar bill

twenty dollar bill

4 Canadian quarters

10 Canadian pennies

1 Canadian dime

2 Canadian nickels

102

MONEY ACTIVITIES

Children's Books

Hoban, Tana. *26 Letters and 99 Cents*. New York: Mulberry Books, 1995.

Holtzman, Caren. *A Quarter from the Tooth Fairy*. New York: Scholastic, 1995.

Leedy, Loreen. *The Monster Money Book*. New York: Holiday House, 1992.

McMillan, Bruce. *Jelly Beans for Sale*. New York: Scholastic, 1996.

Money Activities

Dramatic Play

Make purses and billfolds from construction paper. Fill with coins and paper money for children to use as they role play.

Snack Stand

Serve the milk and snack each day at a selling stand. Provide play money with which children purchase their snacks.

Sorting Change

Provide a muffin tin and allow children to sort real or play coins. A sorting bank allows children to fill each column full of coins.

Store

Set up a store with supplies children bring from home. Use a toy cash register in the area with lots of play money in it. Provide money for children to use when role playing.

What's Underneath?

Place several different coins between two sheets of tinfoil. Have children press the foil smooth to try to determine what coins are in between.

Graph Activities

Candy

Count m & m's® as a group. Graph the amount of each color on a blank graph.
Give each child 12–15 m & m's® and have them graph the results.

Floor Graphs

Use masking tape on the tile or on the carpet to make a large graph.

Use colored masking tape on a plastic drop cloth to make graphs of various sizes and shapes.

Shoes

Determine the different kinds of shoes children have and graph them on a floor graph—sneakers, sandals, boots, lace-up shoes.

How Many in Your Family?

Have children count the number of people in their immediate family. Each child fills in the appropriate box to show the number of members in his or her family. When completed, ask children questions to provide exercises in reading graphs. How many families have four people? How many families have three people? Etc.

TLC10191 Copyright © Teaching & Learning Company, Carthage, IL 62321-0010

105

TLC10191 Copyright © Teaching & Learning Company, Carthage, IL 62321-0010

MATH PORTFOLIOS

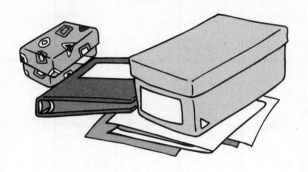

Portfolio Use

A portfolio is a collection of important papers. Portfolios serve as useful tools for teachers to compare an individual student's work over a period of time and when having parent conferences.

Containers for Portfolios

stapled contents with cover

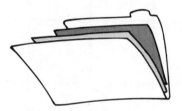

file folders

expanded folders

three-ring folders

student-decorated boxes

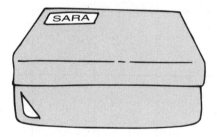

plastic file boxes

MATH PORTFOLIOS

Purpose of Math Portfolios

Math portfolios provide evidence of a student's ability and progress in mathematics.

Items to Include in Math Portfolios

Portfolios should contain a variety of math work papers and tests over a period of time. Ideally one or two papers per week is a manageable amount. It is important that all papers show dates when the work was completed. Work pages and tests should be arranged in sequence prior to meeting with parents. This easily shows the progress, or lack of, that a student has made.

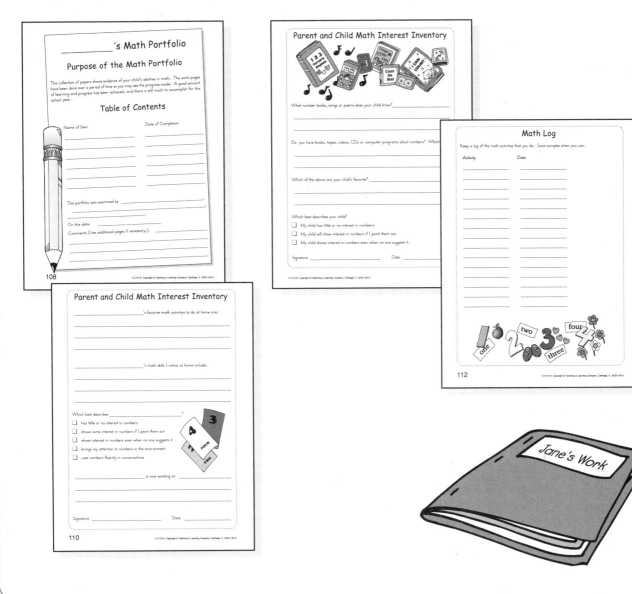

_____'s Math Portfolio

Purpose of the Math Portfolio

This collection of papers shows evidence of your child's abilities in math. The work pages have been done over a period of time so you may see the progress made. A good amount of learning and progress has been achieved, and there is still much to accomplish for this school year.

Table of Contents

Name of Item   Date of Completion

_____   _____

_____   _____

_____   _____

_____   _____

_____   _____

_____

This portfolio was examined by _____,

_____,

_____.

On this date: _____

Comments (Use additional pages if necessary.): _____

_____

_____

_____

Parent and Child Math Interest Inventory

What number books, songs or poems does your child know? _____

_____

_____

Do you have books, tapes, videos, CDs or computer programs about numbers? Which ones?

_____

_____

Which of the above are your child's favorite? _____

_____

_____

Which best describes your child?

☐ My child has little or no interest in numbers.

☐ My child will show interest in numbers if I point them out.

☐ My child shows interest in numbers even when no one suggests it.

Signature _____ Date _____

Parent and Child Math Interest Inventory

_____'s favorite math activities to do at home are:

_____

_____

_____

_____'s math skills I notice at home include:

_____

_____

_____

Which best describes _____?

☐ has little or no interest in numbers

☐ shows some interest in numbers if I point them out

☐ shows interest in numbers even when no one suggests it

☐ brings my attention to numbers in the environment

☐ uses numbers fluently in conversations

_____ is now working on _____

_____

_____

Signature _____   Date _____

110

Numbers in Our Room

Name _____ Date _____

Copy some of the numbers in your room.

Math Log

Keep a log of the math activities that you do. Save samples when you can.

Activity	Date	Sample? Circle yes or no.
_____	_____	yes no
_____	_____	yes no
_____	_____	yes no
_____	_____	yes no
_____	_____	yes no
_____	_____	yes no
_____	_____	yes no
_____	_____	yes no
_____	_____	yes no
_____	_____	yes no
_____	_____	yes no
_____	_____	yes no
_____	_____	yes no
_____	_____	yes no
_____	_____	yes no

Number Songs I Know

Number Books I Have Read

Number Nursery Rhymes and Poems I Know

MATH QUICKIES

- ☐ Count the children in class several times a day.
- ☐ Compare your child count to the total enrolled.
- ☐ Post attractive and colorful numbers in the room.
- ☐ Post times with your daily schedule.
- ☐ Make number pocket charts.
- ☐ Post and use a number line.
- ☐ Post TV and radio station call numbers.
- ☐ Look up phone numbers and addresses in phone books.
- ☐ Check the time frequently.
- ☐ Post children's addresses (check for privacy).
- ☐ Post children's phone numbers (check for unlisted ones).
- ☐ Use the teaching clock frequently.

- ☐ Count the blocks as you put them away.
- ☐ Count puzzle pieces before doing the puzzle.
- ☐ Count the number at the table or center.
- ☐ Count out straws, napkins, etc., for snack.
- ☐ Count the crayons in the box.
- ☐ Count the raisins in small boxes.
- ☐ Count the number of candies in individual containers.
- ☐ Count the chocolate chips in a cookie.
- ☐ Count the number of children wearing _____.
- ☐ Count the number of children going on the bus.
- ☐ Count the number of children wearing short sleeves.

116

MATH QUICKIES

☐ Read number stories.

"Three Bears," "Three Billy Goats Gruff"
and "Three Little Pigs"

"The Wolf and the Seven Little Kids"

"How Many Spots Does a Leopard Have?"

"Snow White and the Seven Dwarfs"

☐ Sing number songs.

"This Old Man"

"Six Little Ducks That I Once Knew"

"Three Blind Mice"

"Five Little Speckled Frogs"

"Five Little Ducks Went Swimming
One Day"

"Check the Sesame Street Number Songs"

☐ Use number poems and nursery rhymes.

"One, Two, Buckle My Shoe"

"1, 2, 3, 4, 5, I Caught a Fish Alive"

"Three Little Kittens"

"Five Little Monkeys Jumping on the Bed"

"Five Little Monkeys Sitting in the Tree"

"Ten in the Bed"

"Hickory, Dickory, Dock"

"Baa, Baa, Black Sheep"

"Hot Cross Buns"

"Rub a Dub, Dub"

"Old King Cole"

BIBLIOGRAPHY

Board Books for Young Children and Early Readers

Books	Subjects
Aker, Suzanne. *What Comes in 2's, 3's and 4's?* Aladdin Paperbacks, 1992.	Sets
Anastasio, Dina. *It's About Time.* New York: Grosset and Dunlop, Inc., 1993.	Time
Anholt, Catherine, and Laurence Anholt. *One Two Three, Count with Me.* New York: Puffin Books, 1996.	Miscellaneous
Anno, Mitsumasa. *Anno's Counting Book.* New York: HarperTrophy, 1986.	Miscellaneous
Asbjornsen, Peter Christian. *The Three Billy Goats Gruff.* New York: Harcourt Brace, 1991.	Goats
Axelrod, Amy. *Pigs Will Be Pigs: Fun with Math and Money.* New York: Demco Media, 1997.	Pigs
Baker, Alan. *Two Tiny Mice.* New York: Dial Books for Young Readers, 1991.	Mice
Baker, Alan. *Gray Rabbit's 1, 2, 3.* New York: Kingfisher Books, 1994.	Rabbits
Bang, Molly. *Ten, Nine, Eight.* New York: Tupelo Books, 1998.	Bedtime
Bohdal, Susi. *1, 2, 3 What Do You See?: An Animal Counting Book.* New York: North-South Books, 1997.	Animals
Boon, Emilie. *1, 2, 3 How Many Animals Can You See?* New York: Orchard Books, 1987.	Animals
Boynton, Sandra. *Hippos Go Berserk.* New York: Aladdin Paperbacks, 1996.	Hippos
Boynton, Sandra. *One, Two, Three.* New York: Workman Publishing, 1993.	Animals

118

BIBLIOGRAPHY

Board Books for Young Children and Early Readers

Books	Subjects
Brisson, Pat. *Benny's Pennies*. New York: Yearling Books, 1995.	Money
Brown, Margaret Wise. *The Runaway Bunny*. New York: HarperFestival, 1991.	Bunnies
Brusca, Maria C. *Three Friends: A Counting Book*. New York: Henry Holt, 1995.	Friends, Counting
Brusca, Maria, and Tana Wilson. *Tres Amigos: Un Cuentro Para Contar*. New York: Henry Holt, 1995.	Spanish
Burns, Marilyn. *The Brown Paper School Presents: The I Hate Mathematics! Book*. Boston: Little, Brown & Co., 1976.	General
Burns, Marilyn. *The Greedy Triangle*. New York: Scholastic, 1995.	Geometry
Burns, Marilyn. *Math for Smarty Pants*. Boston: Little, Brown, & Co., 1982.	General
Carle, Eric. *La Oruga May Hambrienta (The Very Hungry Caterpillar)*. Putman Pub. Group, 1994.	Foods, Butterfly
Carle, Eric. *The Very Hungry Caterpillar*. New York: Philomel Books, 1991.	Foods, Butterfly
Chambless, R. *The Real Mother Goose Clock Book*. New York: Cartwheel Books, 1994.	Time
Christelow, Eileen, *Five Little Monkeys Jumping on the Bed*. New York: Clarion Books, 1998.	Monkeys
Christelow, Eileen, *Five Little Monkeys Sitting in a Tree*. New York: Clarion Books, 1993.	Monkeys
Chwast, Seymour. *The Twelve Circus Rings*. Orlando, FL: Harcourt Brace & Co., 1996.	Circus
Cousins, Lucy. *Count with Maisy*. Cambridge, MA: Candlewick Press, 1997.	Mouse
Cousins, Lucy. *Fit-A-Shape Series: Numbers*. Philadelphia, PA: Running Press, 1996.	Numbers
Cousins, Lucy. *Fit-A-Shape Series: Patterns*. Philadelphia, PA: Running Press, 1996.	Patterns
Cousins, Lucy. *Fit-A-Shape Series: Shapes*. Philadelphia, PA: Running Press, 1996.	Shapes
Crews, Donald. *Ten Black Dots*. New York: Mulberry Books, 1995.	General
Cristaldi, Kathryn. *Even Steven and Odd Todd*. New York: Cartwheel Books, 1996.	Numbers
Dee, Ruby. *Two Ways to Count to Ten: A Liberian Folktale*. New York: Henry Holt, 1990.	Numbers
Dodds, Dayle Ann. *The Shape of Things*. Cambridge, MA: Candlewick Press, 1996.	Shapes
Dubin, Jill, and Tessa Krailing. *One, Two, Three*. New York: Barron's Educational Series, 1991.	General
Dudko, Mary Ann. *Baby Bop's Counting Book*. Allen, TX: The Lyons Group, 1993.	Baby Bop
Dunbar, Joyce. *Ten Little Mice*. San Diego: Harcourt Brace, 1992.	Mice

BIBLIOGRAPHY

Board Books for Young Children and Early Readers

Books	Subjects
Edwards, Roberta. *Five Silly Fishermen*. New York: Random House, 1989.	Fish Fishermen
Emberley, Rebecca. *Three Cool Kids*. Boston: Little, Brown & Co., 1998.	General
Enderle, Judith. *Six Creepy Sheep*. Honesdale, PA: Caroline House, Boyds Mills Press, 1992.	Sheep
Friedman, Aileen. *The King's Commissioners*. New York: Scholastic, 1995.	Story
Gedees, Anne. *1, 2, 3*. San Rafael, CA: Cedco Publishing, Co., 1995.	
Geringer, Laura. *A Three Hat Day*. New York: HarperTrophy, 1987.	Hats
Giganti, Paul. *Each Orange Had 8 Slices: A Counting Book*. New York: Greenwillow Books, 1992.	Foods
Grossman, Virginia. *Ten Little Rabbits*. San Francisco: Chronicle Books, 1998.	Rabbits
Harshman, Marc. *Only One*. New York: Cobblehill Books, 1993.	Shapes
Hoban, Tana. *Shapes, Shapes, Shapes*. New York: Mulberry Books, 1996.	Shapes
Holtzman, Caren. *A Quarter from the Tooth Fairy*. New York: Scholastic, 1995.	Money
Hong, Lily Toy. *Two of Everything*. Morton Grove, IL: Albert Whitman & Co., 1993.	Twos
Hooker, Yvonne. *One Green Frog*. New York: Grosset Dunlop, 1989.	Frogs
Hutchins, Pat. *1 Hunter*. New York: William Morrow & Company, 1982.	
Hutchins, Pat. *The Doorbell Rang*. New York: Mulberry Books, 1989.	Cookies

BIBLIOGRAPHY

Board Books for Young Children and Early Readers

Books	Subjects
Jackson, Woody. *Counting Cows*. San Diego: Harcourt Brace & Co., 1995.	Counting Cows
Keenan, Sheila. *The Biggest Fish*. New York: Scholastic, 1996.	Fish
Keller, Holly. *Ten Sleepy Sheep*. New York: William Morrow & Co., 1983.	Sheep Bedtime
Kunhardt, Dorothy. *Pat the Bunny*. New York: Golden Books Pub., 1998.	Bunnies
Leedy, Loreen. *The Monster Money Book*. New York: Holiday House, 1992.	Money
Leedy, Loreen. *2 x 2 = Boo! A Set of Spooky Multiplication Stories*. New York: Holiday House, 1996.	General
Leonard, Marcia. *Counting Kangaroos: A Book About Numbers*. Mahwah, NJ: Troll Associates, 1990.	Kangaroos
Liebler, J. *Frog Counts to 10*. Brookfield, CT: Millbrook, Press, 1995.	Frogs
Long, Lynette. *Domino Addition*. Watertown, MA: Charlesbridge, Pub., 1997.	Adding
MacCarone, Grace. *Monster Math*. New York: Scholastic, 1995.	General
MacCarone, Grace. *The Silly Story of Goldie Locks and the Three Squares*. New York: Cartwheel Books, 1996.	Geometry
Mahy, Margaret. *17 Kings and 42 Elephants*. New York: Dial Books for Young Readers, 1987.	General
Mahy, Margaret. *The Seven Chinese Brothers*. New York: Scholastic, 1992.	General
Marshall, James. *Three Up a Tree*. Puffin, 1994.	Trees
Marzollo, Jean. *Ten Cats Have Hats: A Counting Book*. New York: Scholastic, 1994.	Cats Hats
Mazzola, Frank Jr. *Counting Is for the Birds*. Watertown, MA: Charlesbridge, 1997.	Birds

BIBLIOGRAPHY

Board Books for Young Children and Early Readers

Books	Subjects
Merriam, Eve. *12 Ways to Get to 11*. Aladdin Paperbacks, 1996.	Addition
Morozumi, Atusko. *One Gorilla, Inc.: First American Edition*. Sunburst & Inc., 1993.	Gorilla, Rain forest
Murphy, Chuck. *My First Counting Book*. New York: Scholastic, 1991.	Miscellaneous
Ong, Christina, and Watty Piper. *The Little Engine That Could: Let's Count 1, 2, 3*. Price Stern Sloan Publishers, 1991.	Trains
Paul, Ann Whitford. *Eight Hands Round: A Patchwork Alphabet*. New York: HarperTrophy, 1996.	Geometry
Pienkowski, Jan. *123*. New York: Little Simon, 1998.	Numbers
Pinczes, Elinor. *One Hundred Hungry Ants*. Boston: Houghton	

TLC10191 Copyright © Teaching & Learning Company, Carthage, IL 62321-0010

BIBLIOGRAPHY

Board Books for Young Children and Early Readers

Books	Subjects
Pluckrose, Henry. Math Counts Series: Capacity. Chicago: Children's Press, 1995.	Capacity
Pluckrose, Henry. Math Counts Series: Counting. Chicago: Children's Press, 1995.	Counting
Pluckrose, Henry. Math Counts Series: Length. Chicago: Children's Press, 1995.	Length
Pluckrose, Henry. Math Counts Series: Numbers. Chicago: Children's Press, 1995.	Numbers
Pluckrose, Henry. Math Counts Series: Patterns. Chicago: Children's Press, 1995.	Patterns

BIBLIOGRAPHY

Board Books for Young Children and Early Readers

Books	Subjects
Pluckrose, Henry. Math Counts Series: Shape. Chicago: Children's Press, 1995.	Geometry
Pluckrose, Henry. Math Counts Series: Size. Chicago: Children's Press, 1995.	Size
Pluckrose, Henry. Math Counts Series: Time. Chicago: Children's Press, 1995.	Time
Pluckrose, Henry. Math Counts Series: Weight. Chicago: Children's Press, 1995.	Weight

BIBLIOGRAPHY

Board Books for Young Children and Early Readers

Books	Subjects
Raffi. *Five Little Ducks*. New York: Crown, 1992.	Ducks
Rann, Toni (Ed.). *My First Look at Numbers*. New York: Random House, 1990.	Numbers
Reasoner, Charles. *Number Munch*. Los Angeles, CA: Price Stern Sloan, 1993.	Animals
Reid, Margarette. *The Button Box*. Puffin, 1995.	Counting, Buttons
Ricklen, Neil. *Baby's 1, 2, 3*. New York: Simon & Schuster, 1997.	Miscellaneous
Rocklin, Joanne. *How Much Is That Guinea Pig in the Window?* New York: Scholastic, 1995.	Money
Schreiber, Anne. *Slower Than a Snail*. New York: Scholastic, 1995.	Time Snails

BIBLIOGRAPHY

Board Books for Young Children and Early Readers

Books

Schwartz, David. *How Much Is a Million?* New York: Mulberry Books, 1993.

Schwartz, David. *If You Made a Million?* New York: Mulberry Books, 1994.

Sierra, Judy. *Counting Crocodiles.* San Diego: Harcourt Brace, 1997.

Singer, Muff. *Puppy Says 1, 2, 3.* New York: Readers Digest Young Families, Inc., 1993.

Smith, Maggie. *Counting Our Way to Maine.* New York: Orchard Books, 1995.

Souza, Dorothy M. *Eight Legs.* Minneapolis: Carolrhoda Books, 1991.

Subjects

Numbers

Numbers

Counting

Crocodiles

Puppies

Counting

States

Insects

BIBLIOGRAPHY

Board Books for Young Children and Early Readers

Books	Subjects
Stoeke, Janet M. *One Little Puppy Dog*. New York: Dutton, 1998.	Counting
Sturges, Philemon. *Ten Flashing Fireflies*. New York: North-South Books, 1997.	Insects
Strickland, Paul. *One Bear, One Dog*. New York: Dutton Children's Books, 1997.	Bears
	Dogs
Tildes, Phyllis. Counting on Calico. Watertown, MA: Charlesbridge, Pub., 1995.	Counting
Tofts, Hannah. *I Eat Fruit!* New York: Larousse Kingfisher Chambers, 1998.	Counting, Fruits
Tofts, Hannah. *I Eat Vegetables!* New York: Larousse Kingfisher	Counting, Vegetables

BIBLIOGRAPHY

oard Books for Young Children and Early Readers

Books	Subjects
Tompert, Ann. *Grandfather Tang's Story*. New York: Dragonfly, 1997.	General
Viorst, Judith. *Alexander and the Terrible, Horrible, No Good, Very Bad Day* (audiocassette). New York: HarperAudio, 1996.	Money
Voss, Gi. *Museum Numbers*. Boston: Boston Museum of Fine Arts, 1994.	Counting
Voss, Gi. *Museum Shapes*. Boston: Boston Museum of Fine Arts, 1993.	Shapes
Walsh, Ellen Stole. *Mouse Count*. New York: Red Wagon, 1995.	Mice
Walton, Rick. *How Many? How Many? How Many?* Cambridge, MA: Candlewick Press, 1996.	Counting
Wane, Heather. *10 Little Bunnies*. New York: Golden Books, 1998.	Bunnies
Wegman, William. *1, 2, 3*. New York: Hyperion Press, 1995.	Dogs